ANTON

Cornwall

National Trust

Acknowledgements

This is a revised version of the guide first published in 1992, supplemented with new photographs by Andreas von Einsiedel, John Hammond and Stephen Robson, commissioned by the National Trust Photographic Library. It is indebted to the previous edition by Michael Trinick, and to F. E. Halliday's biographies of Richard Carew and the Carew family. The chapter on the garden also draws heavily on the unpublished accounts of Crispin Gill and the Head Gardener, Val Anderson. The picture entries have been compiled by Alastair Laing, the Trust's Adviser on Pictures and Sculpture. The furniture entries have been updated by Christopher Rowell, the Trust's Furniture Curator. Sir Richard Carew Pole has put me right on various points. I am also grateful to the following for their help: James Bettley, John Harris, the late Helena Hayward, Joan Richardson, and, most particularly, to Jeremy Pearson.

Oliver Garnett, 2002

Further reading

CORNFORTH, John, 'Antony House, Cornwall I, II', *Country Life*, 9, 16 June 1988, pp. 162–6, 252–7; ELDRIDGE, Tom, 'A Woodland Garden in Cornwall', *Country Life*, 17 October 1963, pp. 978–82; HALLIDAY, F.E., *Richard Carew of Antony: The Survey of Cornwall*, Andrew Melrose, 1953; HALLIDAY, F.E., ed., *A Cornish Chronicle: The Carews of Antony from Armada to Civil War*, David & Charles, 1967; HARRIS, John, 'The Prideaux Collection of Topographical Drawings', *Architectural History*, vii, 1964, p. 23, pl. 1–3; HUSSEY, Christopher, 'Antony House, Cornwall I, II', *Country Life*, lxxiv, 19, 26 August 1933, pp. 172–7, 202–6; ROWSE, A.L., 'Richard Carew Antiquary', *Court and Country: Studies in Tudor Social History*, Harvester Press, 1987, pp. 242–77; TILDEN, Philip, *True Remembrances*, Country Life, 1954, p. 168.

Illustrations: English Heritage/Mr Prideaux-Brune p. 33; National Trust pp. 24, 34, 39 (top); NT/Cameracraft pp. 20, 21, 31 (bottom right), 35; NT/Robert Chapman pp. 37 (top left), 39 (bottom); National Trust Photographic Library/Brian and Nina Chapple p. 25; NTPL/Derek Croucher pp. 4, 26 (top left), 38; NTPL/Andreas von Einsiedel pp. 1, 5, 7, 9, 10, 11, 13, 14, 16, 18, 23, 37 (bottom right); NTPL/John Hammond front cover, pp. 12, 17, 29, 30, 31 (top left), 32, 36, 40, back cover; NTPL/Stephen Robson p. 26 (bottom right).

High-quality prints from the extensive and unique collections of the National Trust Photo Library are available at www.ntprints.com

Published by National Trust (Enterprises) Ltd

If you would like to become a member or make a donation, please telephone 0844 800 1895 (minicom 0844 800 4410); write to The National Trust, PO Box 39, Warrington, WA5 7WD; or see our website at www.nationaltrust.org.uk

Designed by James Shurmer (6 10)

Printed by Hawthornes for National Trust (Enterprises) Ltd, Heelis, Kemble Drive, Swindon, Wilts SN2 2NA on Cocoon Silk made from 100% recycled paper

(*Front cover*) Nicholas Condy's early 19th-century watercolour of the Hall

(*Back cover*) Elizabethan 'black work' embroidery in the Library

(*Opposite*) Satyrs' heads decorate the legs of an early 18th-century walnut table in the Tapestry Room

CONTENTS

A HOUSE FULL OF FACES

There have been Carews at Antony since the early 15th century. Six centuries later, there are Carews living here still. And portraits of them look down from every wall.

Hanging on the right-hand wall of the Entrance Hall is an image of RICHARD CAREW, author of *The Survey of Cornwall* (1602), which provides a delightfully intimate picture of his native county in the Elizabethan era. His memory is kept alive by this portrait and by his writings, as the Latin motto on the picture ('life in spite of death') hoped.

Over the fireplace opposite is a poignant portrait of Charles I at his trial in 1648, his beard turned prematurely grey by the traumas of the Civil War. The King was executed a month after it was painted. The Civil War tore apart the Carew family. JOHN CAREW supported Parliament, but his half-brother, ALEXANDER, backed the Crown. The full-length portrait of Alexander in the Library still bears the scars of being slashed from its frame by members of the family who were outraged at his initial support of Parliament. Worse followed: both John and Alexander were executed for their beliefs.

On the main stairs hangs Sir WILLIAM CAREW, who began building the present house in 1720, with money inherited by his wife, Anne Coventry. He commissioned a plain, but beautifully proportioned, classical house of grey Pentewan stone that glitters like silver in the sunlight. Antony has been little altered since, and stands out as one of the most attractive country houses in Cornwall.

The setting is even more breathtaking. The house sits high above the estuary of the River Lynher, with grassy vistas sweeping down from terraced flower-beds between clumps of trees to the water.

Subsequent generations have enriched the house with many portraits (chiefly from the ancient Pole family), historic tapestries, furniture and china. The present baronet, Sir Richard Carew Pole, keeps these creative traditions alive, commissioning portraits of the next generation of the family, and ambitious new sculpture for the garden.

The catalogue of the North Mymms Park collection, sold by Christie's 24–26 Sept 1979, reveals its very high quality, which in terms of furniture mainly consisted of Continental pieces.

KEY DATES

1602 Richard Carew publishes his *Survey of Cornwall.*

1644 Sir Alexander Carew executed for treason.

1660 John Carew executed for treason.

1720 Sir William Carew begins building the present Antony House.

1792 Humphry Repton presents his scheme for remodelling the garden and park in informal style.

1874 William Henry Pole-Carew adds new porch.

1905 Sir Reginald Pole-Carew builds new wing (demolished in the 1940s).

1961 Sir John Carew Pole gives Antony to the National Trust.

The south front

The walls of the Main Stairs are lined with family portraits

TOUR OF THE HOUSE

THE ENTRANCE PORCH

The *porte-cochère* and entrance porch were added to the south front by William Henry Pole-Carew in the mid-19th century to provide a covered carriage porch and to make the Hall less draughty.

SCULPTURE

ENGLISH, 19th-century
William Henry Pole-Carew (1811–88)

ENGLISH, 19th-century
Frances Anne Pole-Carew (d. 1902)
Wife of William Henry Pole-Carew.

ALEXANDER MUNRO (1825–71)
William Lyttelton Pole-Carew (1856–61)
Their youngest son, who died aged six.

VIOLET, DUCHESS OF RUTLAND (1856–1937)
Lady Beatrice Pole-Carew (1876–1952)
Bronze
Daughter of the 3rd Marquess of Ormonde and wife of Sir Reginald Pole-Carew.

A mid-19th-century carved alabaster urn.

JOHN, CHEERE
Shepherd and *Shepherdess*
Two painted lead mid-18th-century statues

FURNITURE

A set of late 18th-century oak hall-chairs, bearing the Pole crest.

MILITARIA

The cannonballs were found near the house and probably date from the unsuccessful siege of Plymouth by the army of Charles I in 1642. A standard compass binnacle cover from HMS *Exeter*, which was seriously damaged during the Battle of the River Plate in 1939.

THE HALL

The room is panelled in stained oak, as are the other principal rooms on the ground floor, except for the Library.

PICTURES

FIREPLACE WALL:

Manner of HENRI GASCARS (c.1635–1701)
Charles II (1630–85)
Shown in his Garter robes.

CORNELIS JONSON (1593–1661)
Portrait of an Unknown Boy, inscribed as the Earl of Effingham
Signed and dated 1638

EDWARD BOWER (active 1629–66/7)
Charles I at his Trial
Signed: *Edw. Bower/Att Temple barr/fecit. 1648*

ENGLISH, 1670s
Aubrey de Vere, 20th Earl of Oxford, KG (1626/7–1703)
One of the six lords who went to The Hague to invite Charles II to return to England.

After CORNELIS JONSON (1593–1661)
Lord Keeper Coventry (1578–1639/40)
Great-great-grandfather of Lady Anne Carew (see below).

FAR WALL:

MICHAEL DAHL (1656/9–1743)
Gilbert Coventry, 4th Earl of Coventry (c.1668–1719)
Signed: *Mich^l. Dahl pinx:/1714*
Father-in-law of Sir William Carew, 5th Bt. Painted in his peer's robes, shortly after his succession in 1712. It was this unexpected event that transformed the prospects of Sir William, who was set to marry his only daughter and heir, and made possible the building of the new house at Antony.

The Hall

Attributed to MICHAEL DAHL (1656/9–1743)
Lady Anne Carew (1695/6–1733)
Daughter and heir of the 4th Earl of Coventry, married to Sir William Carew, 5th Bt, in 1713.

FACING FIREPLACE:

JACOB HUYSMANS (c.1633–c.1696)
Sir William Morice, MP, PC of Werrington (1602–76)
Helped to win over General Monck to the restoration of Charles II in 1660. His granddaughter Mary became the third wife of Sir John Carew, 3rd Bt.

WILLIAM HOARE (1707–99)
Philip Yorke, 1st Earl of Hardwicke (1690–1764)
Painted in 1763, in his robes as Lord High Chancellor. His granddaughter Jemima married Reginald Pole-Carew in 1784.

?MARCUS GHEERAERTS the Younger (1561/2–1635/6)
Portrait of a Nobleman
A portrait perhaps of Lord Norreys.

ENGLISH, 1586
Richard Carew (1555–1620)
Painted in 1586 in his chains of office as High Sheriff and Deputy-Lieutenant of Cornwall. The emblem (top left) shows a diamond on an anvil surviving the blows of a hammer, with the Italian motto 'Who is truthful will endure'. His book is inscribed *Invita [mor]te vita* ('Life in spite of death').

FURNITURE

The Hall floor has a border with a diamond fret pattern enlivened by dark-stained and ebonised oak inlays. All the ground-floor rooms are wainscoted with bolection mouldings and fielded panels to match. This gives the house considerable warmth

7

and acts as a foil to the furniture, paintings and tapestries.

The pair of elaborate made-up carved armchairs in 17th-century style, c.1860, 'flanking the chimney-piece', is a testament to the antiquarian treatment of Antony in the 17th century.

A carved oak chest, Rouen, 16th century, with a 19th-century replacement English top. The front – centred by its original decorative iron lock and hasp – is decorated with the *Virgin and Child* (centre) flanked by two pairs of allegorical figures or 'virtues', separated by turned pilasters, and supported on a lower rectangular section. It is traditionally supposed to have come from the early house at Antony, and has certainly been in the Hall since c.1820 when it was depicted in the foreground of one of Condy's interior views

A set of eight finely carved mahogany chairs and two sofas covered in bluey green stamped velvet, c.1730 (partly shown in the Hall).

CERAMICS

A pair of large Chinese lidded porcelain vases, in *famille rose* colours, Qianlong period (1736–95). A pair of porcelain storks, Qianlong. A pair of Chinese porcelain storks, 20th-century. A tureen and plates from a soft-paste porcelain service made at the Cozzi factory in Venice between 1775 and 1780.

CLOCK

Ebony-cased bracket clock, late 17th- or early 18th-century.

THE INNER HALL

STAIRCASE

The refined oak staircase with its turned balusters, three to each step, with carved ends, Corinthian columns at the angles, and its original branched glass candle globes, was fitted in 1724. On the landing is parquet laid in the same diamond pattern drawn by John Evelyn as a great curiosity in 1679.

Visitors are asked not to use the stairs, which are fragile. The paintings on the stairs are best viewed from the first floor, and are described on p. 20.

PICTURES

WALL FACING WINDOWS:

JUAN PANTOJA DE LA CRUZ (c.1553–1608)
'Countess Pallavicino'
If rightly named, it may depict Lavinia Biglia of Milan, a lady of the bedchamber to the Queen of Spain, who in 1579 enabled her to marry Orazio Pallavicino, marchese di Scipione (d. 1613). Burns Collection, inherited by Sir John Carew Pole's wife, Cynthia Burns, a great-niece of the American financier J. P. Morgan.

ENGLISH, ?18th-century
Sir Nicholas Carew of Beddington, KG (d. 1539)
From a cadet branch of the family. A close friend of Henry VIII when they were both young men, but later beheaded for expressing discontent with the regime.

MILITARIA

A Commanding Officer's Colour and a Company Colour of the 2nd Battalion, Coldstream Guards, and two drums and bugles of the regiment. Sir John Carew Pole and his father both had distinguished careers in the Coldstream Guards. Two Union flags and a silk family flag. Four 17th-century pikes, dating from the Civil War.

CLOCKS

An 18th-century longcase clock in japanned case, movement by J. Windmills, London. A French bracket clock in an early 18th-century Boulle and ormolu case.

FURNITURE

From the time the house was built in the 1720s are several side tables in the Hall and Inner Hall: a pair of white marble-topped mahogany cabriole leg and club-footed tables, and a six-legged walnut side table, with mottled pink [Cornish?] marble top and an unusual shaped frieze, all of c.1730, as are another contemporary, but less distinguished, pair of marble-topped oak side tables.

A Boulle bracket clock, with good gilt bronze mounts, surmounted by a figure of Time with his scythe, c.1715–20 (its original wall bracket en-suite is in store) stands on the large six-legged side table beneath the Staircase in the Inner Hall.

A 16th-century oak court cupboard said to have come from the original house at Antony, and bearing the initials WC for William Carew.

A set of five Charles II walnut-framed chairs.

CERAMICS

A set of three Japanese Imari plates, probably 17th-century. Two Kangxi porcelain plates. A pair of late 19th-century Chinese porcelain vases, a pair of modern Chinese *cloisonné* geese and a pair of Ming figures.

GLASS

Cast optical glass sculpture on basalt, by Colin Reid, 1999.

The display in the Inner Hall includes a pair of probably 17th-century Japanese Imari plates

THE DINING ROOM

In 1809 the room was enlarged at the south end by taking in part of the Inner Hall. The south wall was later returned to its original position.

PICTURES

WEST (FIREPLACE) WALL:

JOHN VANDERVAART (1653–1727)
Two spaniels and a jay in a landscape
Gilbert, 4th Earl of Coventry paid the artist £10 15s for this picture in 1714.

JOHN WOOTTON (c.1682–1764)
Gilbert 4th Earl of Coventry with two huntsmen in a landscape
Signed
Bought in 1714 by Coventry, one of Wootton's earliest patrons.

EAST WALL:

JAN WYCK (1645–1700) and JOHN VANDERVAART (1653–1727)
Gilbert (4th Earl of) Coventry in the hunting field
Signed
Begun by Wyck in 1699 and completed after his death by Vandervaart.

SOUTH WALL:

JAN WEENIX (1642–1719)
Still-life of dead poultry, with a parrot and spaniel, in a park

FURNITURE

A pair of mahogany cabriole-legged and club-footed tables with black marble tops veined in white, together with two giltwood pier tables with Breche Violette marble tops, on cabriole legs, c.1715, finely carved and with punching in the gesso.

Around a late 19th-century mahogany dining table (made for North Mymms) stand six carved mahogany chairs and a pair of armchairs, of different Gothick/Rococo patterns, c.1760. The armchairs are of superb quality with unusually elaborate Gothick splats, and the legs are decorated to match, incorporating niches among relief fretwork.

CLOCK

A walnut longcase clock by Thomas Parker of Dublin, dated 1798.

GLASS

Largely from the Waterford factory in Ireland, most dating from the early 19th century.

SILVER

A 19th-century nef, a silver model of a 16th-century man-of-war.

THE SALOON

The Saloon mirrors the Hall, occupying the central position on the ground floor of the north front. From the three windows there are beautiful views over the garden to the estuary of the River Lynher.

PICTURES

WEST (FIREPLACE) WALL:

After VAN DYCK (1599–1641)
James Stuart, 1st Duke of Richmond and 4th Duke of Lennox (1612–55) as Paris
Kinsman and favourite of Charles I. The original is in the Louvre.

Sir JOSHUA REYNOLDS (1723–92)
Piping Shepherd Boy
In its day, one of Reynolds's most popular 'fancy pictures'. The painter Benjamin Robert Haydon thought it 'the completest bit of a certain expression in the world'.

Attributed to ENOCH SEEMAN (1692–1749)
Sir Watkin Williams-Wynn, 3rd Bt, MP (1692–1749)
Sir Watkin was a notorious Jacobite, who reputedly gave this portrait to his fellow-Jacobite Sir William Carew to commemorate their pact to raise Wales, Devon and Cornwall for the Stuart cause. Not by Hudson, despite the inscription.

JOHN CLEVELEY (active 1726–77)
Dutch ships in choppy seas
Initialled and dated 1758

EAST WALL:

JOHN CLEVELEY (active 1726–77)
Dutch ships going before the wind
Signed: *I. Clevely 1758*

CHRISTOPHER LE BRUN, RA (b.1951)
Oh! Death will find me
Commissioned by Sir Richard Carew Pole and inspired by this sonnet by Rupert Brooke:

Oh! Death will find me, long before I tire
Of watching you; and swing me suddenly
Into the shade and loneliness and mire
Of the last land! There waiting patiently,

One day, I think, I'll feel a cool wind blowing,
See a slow light across the Stygian tide,
And hear the Dead about me stir, unknowing,
And tremble. And I shall know that you have died,

And watch you, a broad-browed and smiling
    dream,
Pass, light as ever, through the lightless host,
Quietly ponder, start, and sway, and gleam –
Most individual and bewildering ghost! –

The Saloon

The Saloon in the early 19th century; watercolour by Nicholas Condy

And turn and toss your brown delightful head
Amusedly, among the ancient Dead.

After VAN DYCK (1599–1641)
Sir Kenelm Digby (1603–65) with a sunflower
Inscribed: OMNIS IN HOC SUM
Diplomat, scientist, author and close friend of Van Dyck. The sunflower and motto ('In this I am all') are allusions to royal favour.

Attributed to WILLEM VAN DE VELDE the Younger (1633–1707)
Ships in a storm
A drawing by Van de Velde, showing the same main ship in calmer seas, is on the piano.

SOUTH WALL:

Sir JOSHUA REYNOLDS (1723–92)
Thomas, 8th Earl of Westmorland (1700–71)
Painted shortly before he succeeded to the title, on the death of his distant cousin in 1762. Inherited, like the next picture, from the collection of Mrs Arthur James, of Coton House, Warwickshire.

Sir JOSHUA REYNOLDS (1723–92)
John, 9th Earl of Westmorland (1728–74)
The son of the 8th Earl, painted in 1764. The house in the background is probably Brympton d'Evercy in Somerset.

FURNITURE

The dropfront secrétaire, c.1680–90 then called a 'scriptor' is in the style of marquetry associated with the Dutch London-based cabinetmaker, Gerrit Jensen (active 1660s–d.1715).

The pair of carved and gilt gesso pier tables, c.1715 is not en-suite with the pair of carved and gilt gesso pier glasses with shaped arched tops, bevelled glass borders, and pierced anthemion crestings, c.1715.

A Bechstein grand piano, 1893/4.

The crystal chandelier was made in London, c.1840.

CERAMICS

Two late 18th-century Staffordshire pottery cockerels. A Chinese blue-and-white Krak porcelain bowl. A pair of hexagonal Worcester porcelain vases, decorated with panels of exotic birds against a blue ground, dating from the time of the factory's founder, Dr John Wall (1751–76). A set of three Worcester porcelain vases with similar decoration on a blue ground (1751–76).

THE TAPESTRY ROOM

CHIMNEYPIECE

The smoky grey marble chimneypiece, with its inset tripartite looking-glass, was made for the room when the house was built. The fireback is dated 1636.

TAPESTRIES

WEST WALL:

A Soho tapestry depicting a harvesting scene. It was made specially for the house, but had been sold and was bought back by Sir John Carew Pole in 1971.

OTHER WALLS:

These three tapestries show incidents from the life of the Greek philosopher Diogenes. Probably from the Soho factory, late 17th- or early 18th-century.

FURNITURE

A marquetry and gilt bronze bureau, German? c.1760 (on the pier) is typical of North Mymms taste, and is from the house. It is in the style of BVRB (Bernard II van Risamburgh, maître-ébéniste before 1730; b. after 1696–d.c.1766) and Adrien Faizelot-Delorme (maître-ébéniste 1748; active–1783). BVRB's gilt bronze mounts on furniture of this kind are indeed comparable, as are Delorme's, and Delorme in particular went in for pronounced arabesques in his marquetry. However, there is something very Germanic about the pronounced bombé shape, and the arabesques of the marquetry are typically German. The mounts all seem to be in a similar style (ie Louis XV Rococo) except for the Boulle style mount on the lid, which could well be a later addition. Above it is a particularly heavy finely chased rocaille mount, which again suggests Germany.

Two outstanding parcel gilt walnut cabriole-legged side tables, c.1720–30, one with a [Cornish?] pink marble top, the other with a black marble top veined with white, are carved and gilded at the knees with Indians wearing headdresses and with stylised satyrs' masks.

A late 17th-century-style carved oak open armchair with later velvet and silk embroidered upholstery, probably French.

A late 17th-century-style settee with carved oak frame upholstered with later silk and velvet.

An extremely finely inlaid single-pedestal tripod card table, c.1685. The two-flapped folding top is decorated with so-called 'seaweed' marquetry in holly, olive and rosewood. The border is inlaid to suggest seaweed, thus emphasising the reason for the generic name of this distinctive style of inlay. The interior, lined with greeny-blue silk velvet, also retains its original woven silver tape borders. This is a rare survival in almost mint condition: a star piece of Anglo-Dutch furniture in the style of Gerrit Jensen (active 1660s–d.1715).

Heads of Mexican Indians are carved on the legs of a walnut table attributed to John Channon in the Tapestry Room

An early 18th-century walnut and gilt table, with black marble top. The cabriole legs are carved at the knees with satyrs' masks in gilt and terminate in elaborately carved hoofed feet. Again by John Channon.

A pair of Chippendale mahogany armchairs, upholstered in light biscuit ground *gros* and *petit point* needlework in a floral design.

A set of four Dutch 18th-century marquetry chairs upholstered in blue velvet.

The giltwood eight-branch chandelier, Paris, *c.*1725: by tradition this came – via North Mymms Park – from Hamilton Palace, Lanarkshire, Scotland and may be identifiable with lot 647 in the legendary Hamilton Palace 17-day sale held at Christie's, London, on 17 June–28 July 1882 (by order of the 12th Duke of Hamilton):

The Tapestry Room

27 June 1882 (6th day): 647 A CHANDELIER FOR EIGHT LIGHTS, carved and gilt wood, designed by Buhl (the royal ébéniste, André-Charles Boulle, 1642–1732)

Taken from the Catalogue of the Collection of Pictures, Works of Art and Decorative Objects ... the property of his Grace The Duke of Hamilton, K.T... Christie's, London, 1882.

This lot is the only possible one in the 1882 catalogue (though the Antony chandelier may have been bought from Hamilton Palace later). The Antony chandelier is certainly French in style, which is hardly surprising given that most of the furniture at Hamilton Palace was bought by the 10th Duke, a great francophile collector of French furniture. It is unlike the rare English giltwood chandeliers of this date, and indeed French giltwood chandeliers are also extremely unusual. So this is a great rarity. One of Boulle's two published designs for eight-branch chandeliers (presumably intended to be made in gilt bronze) is closer than the other to the Antony chandelier, which is more Rococo in style. It seems to be on the cusp between the Régence (1715–23) and the magnificent Rococo productions of Caffieri (in gilt bronze). The lambrequin canopied top of the chandelier seems to derive from Bérain-esque ornament of around 1700, but the overall flowing shape looks forward to the Caffieri gilt bronze chandeliers in the Wallace Collection, London.

CLOCK

An inlaid walnut longcase clock, by the London maker Benjamin Merriman, c.1690.

CERAMICS

A large collection of figures forming a Ming army, Chinese (1368–1644), purchased by Sir Richard and Lady Carew Pole in 1996.

CARPET

An Aubusson carpet, made for Sir John's mother, Lady Beatrice Pole-Carew. The border echoes the trailing vine pattern of a rare piece of Elizabethan embroidery on display in the Library.

MINIATURES

A collection of Butler family miniatures, largely mid- to late 19th-century.

LACE FANS

Black lace fan. Brussels *point de gaze* lace on mother-of-pearl sticks, which belonged to Lady Constance Leveson Gower, daughter of the 2nd Duke of Sutherland. White lace fan. Brussels *point de gaze* lace fan, which belonged to Harriet, Duchess of Sutherland, Mistress of the Robes to Queen Victoria and mother of the above.

THE LIBRARY

The Library has been altered from its original design in three ways. Firstly, the wall at the north end of the room, which once divided it from the central passage that ran the full length of the house from west to east, has been removed. Secondly, the pine panelling was stripped of its original finish in the 1930s to make a sympathetic background to the fine collection of books from Shute in east Devon. And thirdly, the library was furnished to function as a study in the 19th century.

BOOKS

The Library contains not only the best of the books from Antony, but also much of the outstanding Shute collection. A large number of the Shute books were collected by Sir Courtenay Pole, 2nd Bt, in the late 17th century. Their choice and arrangement was carried out by Charles Henderson, the Cornish historian, in the 1920s. The books are largely on history, travel or military subjects.

PICTURES

WEST WALL:

ENGLISH, c.1630
Sir Alexander Carew, 2nd Bt (1608/9–44)
Royalist members of the family are purported to have slashed this portrait from its frame and consigned it to the cellars after the sitter had raised the Cornish militia on the parliamentary side,

The Library

but to have restored it with crude stitches after he had been executed for attempting to surrender St Nicholas Island to the King. He appears dressed for service in the English regiment in Holland; the buff jerkin is preserved alongside the picture.

JACOB HUYSMANS (*c.*1633–*c.*1696)
Anne Morice, Lady Pole (d. 1713/14)
Oval
Youngest daughter of Sir William Morice, and wife of Sir John Pole, 3rd Bt.

NORTH WALL:

ENGLISH, *c.*1690
Thomas, Viscount Deerhurst, later 2nd Earl of Coventry (*c.*1672–1710)
Oval

ENGLISH, *c.*1690
Winifred Edgcumbe (d. 1694)
Oval
Daughter of Piers Edgcumbe of Mount Edgcumbe, first wife of Thomas, 5th Baron (and subsequently 1st Earl of) Coventry, and mother of the 2nd and 4th Earls.

ENGLISH, *c.*1710
'Mr Edgcumbe'
Oval
Evidently an as yet unidentified relative of the foregoing.

ENGLISH, *c.*1690
Supposed portrait of Margaret Jefferies
Reputedly the wife of Sir Thomas Coventry (1574–1606), and mother of Lord Keeper Coventry; but she lived a century before it was painted.

Circle of JOHN CLOSTERMAN (1660–1711)
Sir Richard Carew, 4th Bt (1684–1703)
Oval

Eldest surviving son of the 3rd Baronet, and brother of the 5th Baronet.

EAST WALL:

THOMAS HUDSON (1701–79)
'Mrs Buller'
This is probably Mary Bampfylde, who married Coventry Carew, 6th and last Bt, in 1738. After his death, she married in 1749 Francis Buller, MP (1723–64) of Morval, and lived with him at Antony.

Sir JOSHUA REYNOLDS (1723–92)
James Buller of Morval, MP (1717–65)
Brother-in-law of the above, painted in 1757. His sister, Anne, married Reginald Pole.

PIETER BORSSALAER (active 1644–87)
Admiral Cornelius Tromp (1629–91)
Painted in London for Ambrose Elton in 1675, after Tromp had negotiated the treaty ending the third Anglo-Dutch war.

Circle of JOHN SINGLETON COPLEY (1738–1815)
Colonel Lemon
Related by marriage to James Buller of Morval (above).

GEORGE ROMNEY (1734–1802)
Jemima Pole Carew (1763–1804)
Granddaughter of Lord Chancellor Hardwicke, and first wife (m. 1784) of Reginald Pole-Carew.

SOUTH WALL:

After Sir GODFREY KNELLER, Bt (1646/9–1723)
Sarah, Duchess of Marlborough (1660–1744)
Termagant wife of the great general, and – until their notorious breach – bosom friend of Queen Anne.

After JOHN RUSSELL (1745–1806)
George IV as Prince of Wales (1762–1830)

INNER LIBRARY, WEST WALL:

Attributed to JOHN MICHAEL WRIGHT (1617–94)
Urith Shapcote, Lady Pole (d. 1696)
Daughter of Sir Thomas Shapcote, married in 1649 to Sir Courtenay Pole, 2nd Bt.

Attributed to GERARD SOEST (c.1600–80/1)
Sir William Pole, Kt, MP (1614–48/9)
Eldest son of Sir John Pole, 1st Bt, but predeceased his father. MP for Honiton in the Long Parliament, he fought on the Cavalier side during the Civil War.

The Library in the early 19th century; watercolour by Nicholas Condy

MARY BEALE (1632/3–99)
Sir Courtenay Pole, 2nd Bt, MP (1618/19–95)
Signed and dated 1670
Younger brother of Sir William Pole and husband of Urith Shapcote (both above). Known as 'Sir Chimney Pool' for his introduction of the highly unpopular Hearth Tax (1662).

JOHN RILEY (1646–91)
Anne Morice, Lady Pole (d. 1713/14)
Wife of Sir John Pole, 3rd Bt, and mother of the 4th Baronet.

Manner of MICHAEL DAHL (1656/9–1743)
Sir William Pole, 4th Bt, MP (1678–1741)
Eldest son of the 3rd Baronet and Master of the Household to Queen Anne, 1712–14.

Attributed to JOHN RILEY (1646–91) *c*.1680
? Sir John Pole, 3rd Bt, MP (1649–1707/8)
Much too early to be Sir William Pole, 4th Bt, as labelled. Possibly therefore his father, the 3rd Baronet.

NORTH WALL:

ALLAN RAMSAY (1713–84)
Sir John Pole, 5th Bt (*c*.1733–60)
Signed and dated 1747
Only son of Sir William Pole, 4th Bt. Seen again in the double portrait on the Stairs.

The green glass paperweights in the Library

Attributed to THOMAS BEACH (1738–1806)
Anne, Lady de la Pole
Married Sir John Pole, 6th Bt, 1781.

THOMAS BEACH (1738–1806)
Rev. Edward Pole (1758–1837)
Signed and dated 1794
Second son of Reginald Pole of Stoke Damerel and Anne Buller of Morval.

Miscellaneous silhouettes, plumbago drawings and wax relief portraits, of Bullers and Poles.

EMBROIDERY

A rare example of Elizabethan 'black work', a linen pillowcase embroidered in silk thread in a continuous pattern of trailing vines.

SHELLWORK

An early 18th-century English oval chaplet of shells mounted on wire, encircling the arms of the Coventry family.

FURNITURE

A French Louis XVI style kingwood *bureau plat*, decorated with ormolu mounts.

CLOCKS

A French Boulle clock. A late 19th-century longcase clock in a japanned case, by George Rowning, Newmarket.

CERAMICS

A pair of French faience honey and sweet jars decorated with flowers. A fine collection of glass doorstops and paperweights, mostly made in Nailsea, near Bristol, in the late 19th century.

THE ANTE-ROOM

This small closet and the Garden Hall contain some of the collection of modern pictures formed by Sir Richard Carew Pole. They were mostly painted in the 1980s and 1990s.

THE WEST STAIRS

These stairs, with their counterparts at the other end of the building, were used by the servants going about their work, or by the children ascending to the nurseries on the second floor.

PICTURES

PETER KUHFELD (b. 1952)
The Carew Pole family
Signed and dated 1985
Depicted in the Library.

ENGLISH, early 18th-century
View of Devonport
Showing the buildings put up by Edward Dummer, Surveyor of the Navy, from 1692 onwards.

THE UPSTAIRS LANDING

FURNITURE

On the Upstairs Landing is a Kentian giltwood side table, *c.*1725-30, decorated with a shell in the centre of the frieze, oak garlands, bellflowers, inverse baluster legs, and with a shaped marble top. This typically sculptural table, of Roman inspiration, is reminiscent of similar tables at Wilton House, Wiltshire (Earl of Pembroke).

THE FIRST FLOOR

THE CORRIDOR

PICTURES

NORTH (LEFT-HAND) WALL:

JAMES SANT, RA (1820–1916)
Mary Morgan, Mrs W. H. Burns
Sister of J. P. Morgan, the American banker and collector, and grandmother of Cynthia Burns, Lady Carew Pole.

Sir HUBERT VON HERKOMER, RA (1849–1914)
Walter Hayes Burns
Initialled and dated 1895

The husband of the above. Also American, he worked in the Morgan Bank (now part of Deutsche Morgan Grenfell).

ENGLISH, 17th-century
Sir Amyas Bampfylde, 1st Bt
A prime ancestor of the wife of the last Carew baronet. Buried at North Molton, Devon.

MARY BEALE (1633–99)
Rachel Carew, Mrs Manaton (1669–1705)
Second daughter of Sir John Carew, 3rd Bt. Married in 1690 Ambrose Manaton, MP (1648–96) of Trecarrell and Kilworthy, as his second wife. Said to be the inspiration of Daphne du Maurier's *My Cousin Rachel*.

Manner of Sir ANTHONY VAN DYCK (1599–1641)
Supposed portrait of Lady Bampfylde

THOMAS BEACH (1738–1806)
William, Mary Ann and John de la Pole as children
Signed on cricket-bat: *T. Beach* 1793
The three children of Sir John Pole, 6th Bt, are shown with bats and ball before Shute Barton.

SOUTH WALL:

FLEMISH, *c.*1620
Portrait of an old, bearded man

BENJAMIN WILSON (1721–88)
Sir William Henry Lyttelton, 7th Bt, 1st Baron Lyttelton (1724–1808)
He is portrayed as Governor of South Carolina (1755–62). His daughter, Caroline, was married to Reginald Pole-Carew in 1808. He was a friend of Dr Johnson and Mrs Thrale, and was Ambassador to Portugal in 1766–7 and Commissioner of the Treasury in 1776–82.

GIACOMO AMIGONI (*c.*1682–1752)
Allegory of Charity

JULIAN STORY (1857–1919)
Sir Reginald Pole-Carew (1849–1924)

Sir OSWALD BIRLEY, MC (1880–1952)
Mary Pole-Carew, 1947
Sister of Sir John Carew Pole.

ELLIS ROBERTS (1860–1930)
Lady Beatrice Butler, Lady Pole-Carew (1876–1952)
Daughter of the 3rd Marquess of Ormonde.

William, Mary Ann and John de la Pole; by Thomas Beach, 1793 (First-floor Corridor)

Sir OSWALD BIRLEY, MC (1880–1952)
Cynthia Burns, Lady Carew Pole (d.1977), 1945
First wife of Sir John Carew Pole, 12th Bt.

Sir OSWALD BIRLEY, MC (1880–1952)
Sir Richard Carew Pole, 13th Bt (b. 1938), 1944

Sir OSWALD BIRLEY, MC (1880–1952)
Sir John Carew Pole, 12th Bt, DSO, TD (1902–93), 1944
Birley was a friend of the family and offered to paint Sir John before D-Day during the Second World War. He painted the portrait of Sir John after two sittings in London.

CERAMICS

A pair of Cozzi porcelain ice-pails, *c.*1770–80.

Two Meissen porcelain tureens and stands, *c.*1739–40.

CHANDELIERS

Two Dutch silver chandeliers based on a late 17th-century design found at Knole in Kent.

FURNITURE

A set of six cabriole-legged walnut side chairs, with unusual pierced hearts in the splats, and shell crestings, *c.*1725–30.

THE MAIN STAIRS

PICTURES

WEST WALL:

JOHN KERSEBOOM (active 1680s–1708)
Gilbert, 4th Earl of Coventry (*c.*1668–1719)
Painted in 1694.

Sir GODFREY KNELLER, Bt (1646/9–1723)
Dorothy Keyt, Countess of Coventry (1670–1705)
Signed and dated 1693
Wife of Gilbert, 4th Earl of Coventry. Their only daughter, Anne, married Sir William Carew, 5th Bt, and brought the wealth that made possible the building of Antony.

THOMAS HUDSON (1701–79)
Sir John Pole, 5th Bt (*c.*1733–60) *and Elizabeth Mill, Lady Pole* (1737–58)
Signed and dated 1755
One of Hudson's masterpieces, showing Sir John and his first wife dressed as if for a masquerade.

JOHN RILEY (1646–91)
Sir John Carew, 3rd Bt, MP (1635–92)
Eldest son of the unfortunate Sir Alexander Carew. A moderate Presbyterian, who represented Cornwall in the Convention Parliament of 1660.

JOHN RILEY (1646–91)
Mary Morice, Lady Carew (d. 1698)
Probably painted around the time of her marriage, *c.*1682, to Sir John Carew, 3rd Bt. Mother of the 4th and 5th Baronets.

? Sir JOSHUA REYNOLDS (1723–92)
Reginald Pole (1717–69)
A descendant, through the female line, of Sir John Carew, 3rd Bt. His son, Reginald Pole-Carew, inherited Antony in 1772.

EAST WALL:

Studio of LELY (1618–80)
The Hon. Francis Robartes, MP, FRS
(1649/50–1717/18)
Composer and scientist (Vice-President of the Royal Society). Second son of the 1st Earl of Radnor by his second marriage. His first wife was Sir Courtenay Pole's daughter, Penelope, whom he married in 1678 (see below).

Studio of LELY (1618–80)
Penelope Pole, the Hon. Mrs Francis Robartes (after 1649–before 1686)

THOMAS BEACH (1738–1806)
Sir John William de la Pole, 6th Bt (1757–99)
Signed and dated 1794
Seen in the library of the new house at Shute, plans of which (1787) he holds.

ENGLISH, *c.*1565
Sir Gawen Carew (d. 1583)
Youngest of the four sons of Sir Edmund Carew (1464–1513) of Mohuns Ottery, who had given up the eponymous family barony and castle of Caer Yw in Pembrokeshire.

THOMAS BEACH (1738–1806)
Anne, Lady de la Pole
Signed and dated 1793
Shown on the terrace of Shute.

Manner of GERRIT VAN HONTHORST (1590–1656)
Supposed portrait of Sir John Pole, 3rd Bt, MP (1649–1707/8)
The style is that of around 1650, so this 'ancestor' – and perhaps the very picture itself – must have been concocted for the 6th Bt.

JAMES NORTHCOTE, RA (1746–1831)
Sir William Templer Pole, 7th Bt, DCL (1782–1847)
Shown as a young man on the steps of Shute, with a dog of the same build as in the portrait of the 6th Baronet, his father.

Sir GODFREY KNELLER, Bt (1646/9–1723)
John, Lord Robartes, 1st Earl of Radnor (1606–85)
Signed and dated 1683
Although originally a Parliamentarian and a Presbyterian, Robartes was successively Lord Privy Seal, Lord Lieutenant of Ireland, and Lord President of the Council under Charles II. There are three versions at the sitter's family home, Lanhydrock.

After Sir PETER LELY (1618–80)
Letitia Isabella Smith, Countess of Radnor (c.1630–1714)
The second wife (m. 1646/7) of the 1st Earl of Radnor (see above). Probably a late 19th-century copy of Lely, painted for Sir William de la Pole, 6th Bt.

SOUTH WALL:

EDWARD PENNY (1714–91)
Mary Bampfylde, Lady Carew (d. 1766)
Married in 1738 to Sir Coventry Carew, 6th and last Bt. She subsequently married Francis Buller, MP.

Manner of Sir PETER LELY (1618–80)
John, 4th Baron Coventry (1654–87)
Son of the 3rd Baron, and succeeded by his uncle, subsequently created 1st Earl.

Sir John and Elizabeth, Lady Pole; by Thomas Hudson, 1755 (Main Stairs)

MICHAEL DAHL (1656/9–1743)
Lady Anne (Coventry) Carew
For biography, see p. 7.

MICHAEL DAHL (1656/9–1743)
Sir William Carew, 5th Bt, MP (1689–1744)
Husband of Lady Anne Coventry, and builder of
Antony, around the time that this portrait was
painted.

Attributed to JOHN WOOTTON (c.1682–1764)
Sir Coventry Carew, 6th Bt (1716?–48)
The last Carew baronet, by whose will Antony
passed to Reginald Pole of Stoke Damerel.

THE BEDROOMS

NORTH (LEFT-HAND) SIDE:

THE CHINTZ DRESSING ROOM

PICTURES INCLUDE:

ENGLISH, 17th-century
Sir William Pole (1561–1635)
The antiquary and historian of Devon.

THE CHINTZ BEDROOM

THE RED BEDROOM

PICTURES INCLUDE:

JEAN-BAPTISTE MONNOYER (1636–99)
Three still-lifes with flowers

THE GREEN BEDROOM

PICTURES INCLUDE:

JIM BACON
Sir John Carew Pole, 12th Bt (1902–93)
Dressed as a pageboy to Lord Knollys at the
Coronation of George V, 1911.

SOUTH (RIGHT-HAND) SIDE:

THE PORCH BEDROOM

JOHN SARTORIUS (1759–1828)
Portraits of dogs and horses
Owned by Sir John William de la Pole of Shute at
the beginning of the 19th century.

After GEORGE ROMNEY (1734–1802)
Sir John William de la Pole of Shute and *Anne, Lady
de la Pole*
The originals were sold in 1913–14, and are now
both in museums in the USA.

THE SOUTH BEDROOM

PICTURES INCLUDE:

JOHN WOOTTON (c.1682–1764)
Battle Scene
This may be the picture bought by the Earl of
Coventry in 1706 for £12, when the frame cost an
extra £1.

THE SOUTH DRESSING ROOM

PICTURES INCLUDE:

Several family portraits of members of the Pole
family.

FURNITURE

The Bedroom furniture includes two mahogany
broken pedimented secretaries-cum-chests of
drawers, c.1760; and two mahogany four-post
beds with scalloped canopies (one gilded),
c.1760–65.

PICTURE FRAMES

Many of the Pole (and de la Pole) portraits are in
distinctive giltwood gallery frames with reeded
and 'bound' edges, c.1800. Indeed, many of the
giltwood frames at Antony are notable, including a
set of finely carved ovals, c.1700 above the book-
cases in the Library, which are arranged in roughly
the same order as they were in a series of interior

views (*c*.1840) by Nicholas Condy (*c*.1793–1857). The collection was then strong in Old Masters, arranged in symmetrical tiers (many of which were sold to make room for the Pole portraits inherited in 1926) and something of this spirit was restored through the marriage in 1928 of Sir John Carew Pole, 12th Bt, to Cynthia Burns, great-niece of the great American financier and collector,

J. Pierpont Morgan, which brought to Antony good furniture and pictures from North Mymms Park, near Hatfield, Hertfordshire. Among the North Mymms pictures (Inner Hall) is *Contessa Pallavicino*? by Juan Pantoja de la Cruz (*c*.1553–1608) in a grand gilded Louis XV style frame, late-19th century (the frame probably supplied to North Mymms).

The Porch Bedroom is hung with 18th- and 19th-century horse paintings

THE PARK AND GARDEN

Like most long-established human landscapes, Antony has been shaped by the cycle of fashion. The formal parterres to the north of Sir William Carew's early 18th-century house were swept away in the 1790s by Humphry Repton, who favoured more open and grassy vistas. In the 19th century, formality returned with William Henry Pole-Carew's Yew Walk to the west of the house and Sir Reginald Pole-Carew's immense and elaborate flower garden to the north. In the 1930s new species of rhododendrons were introduced to the woodlands first established by Sir William Carew. After the Second World War the garden was radically simplified, and most of the Victorian flower-beds returned to grass.

THE SOUTHERN APPROACH

The south carriage drive descends firstly through thick woodland, and then along an avenue lined with lime trees, planted in the 1930s, through which can be seen expanses of grass and the

Bird's-eye view of the garden; by Richard Sorrell, dated 1987

The summer garden

wooded hills beyond. The drive still curves gently to meet the south forecourt of the house as Sir William Carew intended.

From the south forecourt a double avenue of Horse Chestnuts planted by Sir Reginald stretches south up a gentle slope to the horizon.

Against the coach-park wall and in many of the borders are Day Lilies (*Hemerocallis*), which produce flowers from May to September. Some are sweetly scented. There are over 600 cultivars at Antony, which holds a National Collection. They were collected by the late Lady Cynthia Carew Pole in the 1960s and '70s, and include several varieties produced at Antony: 'Lady Cynthia', 'Sir John', 'Torpoint', 'Antony House' and 'Cynthia Mary'.

THE SOUTH FORECOURT

In front of the forecourt are the climbing rose 'Iceberg' and the Asian *Clematis orientalis* and *Clematis tangutica*. Trained against the walls in the-

circular lawned area is a richly scented evergreen *Magnolia grandiflora* 'Exmouth', which produces very large flowers throughout the summer.

THE CORK OAK LAWN AND YEW WALK

West of the house a gravel path runs beside the great yew hedge planted in the mid-19th century by William Henry Pole-Carew. To the left are some good trees – mulberries (*Morus nigra*), Black Walnut, London Plane and an immense Cork Oak (*Quercus suber*).

The huge conical yew topiary contains a shady arbour created by Lady Beatrice Pole-Carew so that she could watch tennis on the grass court that formerly lay opposite. Unfortunately, she was so pestered by insects that she only ever used the seat once!

At the end of the walk is an immense temple bell, which was brought back from Burma in

The knot garden

1886 by Sir Reginald Pole-Carew. It is flanked by granite lanterns from Japan, and backed by Asian rhododendrons and magnolias.

A further walk leads off to the right. Following down the path from here around the outside of Repton's walled garden, you come to another planting of magnolias, in this case the deciduous early *Magnolia.* × *soulangeana*, underplanted with primroses and scillas. In the view to the terrace stands a large Gingko tree. Through the ornamental gate by James Horrobin are a sheltered summer garden and a knot garden made by Lady Carew Pole in 1984.

Beyond this formal area are walks down the West Down valley through 18th-century woodland, planted in the 20th century with rhododendrons, magnolias and camellias. Paths lead on along the Lynher foreshore, past the late 18th-century Bath House and around the flanks of Jupiter Hill to end at the 19th-century Broomhill Cottage. The Antony Woodland Garden does not belong to the National Trust, but is maintained and opened by a private trust.

THE NORTH TERRACES AND LAWNS

The terraces to the north of the house have been home to two formal gardens, laid out by Sir William Carew in the early 18th century and Sir Reginald Pole-Carew in the late 19th. Both have now gone, and the scene is very much as Repton would have wanted it in the 1790s. Clumps of ilex first planted about 1760 frame vast expanses of lawn and provide three broad views of the River Lynher and the opposite bank.

On either side of the central steps are plantings of osmanthus, a fragrant evergreen shrub which is very attractive to bees. On the top terrace stand urns copied from the finials on the entrance gates to the forecourt. Large catmint (*Nepeta* 'Six Hills Giant') provides an aromatic blue carpet for borders of 'Iceberg' roses. The rose hedge behind is *Rosa pimpinellifolia*. On the middle terrace, borders of the rugosa rose 'Blanche Double de Coubert' are broken up by the Mexican mock orange blossom (*Choisya ternata*). Asarina grows in crevices in the walls, producing antirrhinum-like pale yellow flowers throughout the summer. The bottom terrace is an attractive mixture of shrubs and herbaceous plants. Sweetly scented *Trachelospermum jasminoïdes* is trained up the red-brick walls. The dovecote is contemporary with the house. Its conical roof is echoed in the bronze fountain commissioned from the sculptor William Pye by Sir Richard Carew Pole.

William Pye's 'Water Cone' fountain complements the shape of the 18th-century dovecote on the North Terraces

THE CAREWS OF ANTONY

The Carews are an ancient family, whose name derives from Caer Yw Castle in Pembrokeshire. They first settled at Antony in the early 15th century, when Sir Nicholas Carew married the heiress Joan Courtenay who inherited the estate from her aunt, Margery, Lady Arundell. Joan outlived her husband, who died in 1447. She divided her numerous manors among their younger sons, giving the fourth, Alexander, the manor of East Antony. From these brothers descend the Carews of Antony, Mohuns Ottery, Haccombe and Crowcombe, who intermarried with all the other leading Cornish families until they ruled the life of the county. As Richard Carew aptly remarked, 'All Cornish gentlemen are cousins'.

We know almost nothing of Alexander Carew's home at Antony. It seems to have stood about half a mile to the east of the present house. The only remains are some Tudor panelling in the Hall and granite slabs now serving as stiles across nearby walls, which are said to have once been used as window mullions.

Carew cousins were prominent in the boisterous court of the young Henry VIII, but it was Alexander's grandson, Wymond (by 1498–1549), who was the first member of his branch of the family to make a mark in national life. Probably through the influence of his brother-in-law, Anthony Denny, who was one of the King's favourites in his later years, Wymond was appointed receiver-general in the household of the Queen, Jane Seymour. He subsequently held similar posts under Anne of Cleves and Catherine Parr.

Wymond's son, Thomas (1526/7–64), set about consolidating the family's position in Cornwall. In 1554 he made a powerful alliance with one of Cornwall's greatest families by marrying Elizabeth Edgcumbe, the daughter of Sir Richard Edgcumbe II, who built Mount Edgcumbe and owned Cotehele, the ancestral family house eight miles up the Tamar from Antony (and also the property of the National Trust). Thomas sold much of the property his father had acquired outside Devon and Cornwall, presumably to raise the money to buy the large Cornish manor of Sheviocke, which still forms part of the Antony estate. In 1563 he was returned as MP for Saltash, the borough across the Lynher that was to remain in the control of the Carews for the next two centuries. Thomas died the following year at the age of only 37, leaving an eight-year-old son, Richard, as his heir.

Of all the many Carews, Richard Carew (1555–1620) was the most remarkable. At about eleven he was sent to Oxford, where he was a contemporary of the antiquary William Camden and the poet-warrior Philip Sidney, whom he considered 'the miracle of our age'. A legal training was a valuable aid for any landowner in the famously litigious county of Cornwall, and so Carew moved to London to study at Clement's Inn, and then, in 1574, at the Middle Temple, where he remained about three years. Like his grandfather, he was a good linguist, teaching himself Greek, German, Dutch, French, Spanish and Italian; Latin he had already acquired at school. According to his son, 'He ever delighted so much in reading for he had none other hindrance, going or riding he would ever have a book and be reading.'

In 1577 Carew married Juliana Arundell, a member of the Trerice branch of this powerful Cornish clan, and they settled into the comfortable existence of Elizabethan country gentry. Carew himself described the life of his class:

They keep liberal, but not costly builded or furnished houses, give kind entertainment to strangers, make even at the year's end with the profits of their living, are reverenced and beloved of their neighbours, live void of factions amongst themselves (at leastwise such as break out into any dangerous excess), and delight not in bravery of apparel.... A gentleman and his wife will ride to make merry with his next neighbour, and after a day or twain those two couples go to a third, in which progress they increase like snowballs, till through their burdensome weight they break again.

Carew's younger brother, George, was a leading lawyer and diplomat at court, but although Carew himself accepted his share of the responsibilities that came with his position, he seems to have done so reluctantly. He sat as MP for Saltash, was a JP and High Sheriff of Cornwall. In 1586 he was Deputy-Lieutenant of the county, responsible for defending the coast against the Spaniards, who remained a real threat throughout the 1590s despite the defeat of the Armada in 1588. In 1586 Carew also had himself painted in his chain of office and holding a book bearing the Latin tag *Invita morte vita* ('Life in spite of death'). These words could hardly have been better chosen, for it is through his writings that Carew's name lives on.

Richard Carew was a scholar and antiquary of quite extraordinary range. He wrote a verse epic based on Tasso and a humorous reworking of Sidney's *Arcadia*, entitled *A Herring's Tail*. His *Examination of Men's Wits* (translated via Italian from the Spanish) was the first systematic attempt since classical times to relate physiology to psychology: baldness, he solemnly concluded, was a sign of imagination. However, his greatest achievement is undoubtedly *The Survey of Cornwall*. 'Long since begun, a great while discontinued, lately reviewed, and now hastily finished', it was published in 1602. The *Survey* not only offers an unrivalled portrait of Elizabethan Cornwall, but also of the author, who emerges as a delightfully sympathetic man: modest, sensible, intensely proud of his native county, plain-spoken, humane within the limits of his age, and always prepared to laugh at his own pedantry. Any subject, however obscure, could stir his insatiable curiosity, from the rules of Cornish wrestling to the best way to pickle a pilchard. At the centre of Carew's world was his beloved fish-pond at Antony, which he celebrated in verses that sum up his outlook on life:

I wait not at the lawyer's gates,
Ne shoulder climbers down the stairs;
I vaunt not manhood by debates,
I envy not the miser's fears;
But mean [moderate] in state, and calm in sprite [spirit],
My fishful pond is my delight.

As Carew grew older, blindness gradually overtook him, but he bore the affliction without complaint, even managing to write a treatise on the subject. At the age of 65 on 6 November 1620 he died peacefully, and appropriately, in his library at Antony. He asked to be buried in Antony church, the funeral to be conducted 'without ripping or mourning garments'.

Carew's son and heir, another Richard (c.1580–1643), was prone to pomposity and hypochondria, but had remarkably sensible and advanced views on education. In the *True and Ready Way to Learn the Latin Tongue* he advocated conversation and reading as preferable to the traditional method of rote instruction in the rules of grammar. He was also the best bee-keeper in Cornwall. However, his faith was that of the early 17th-century puritan. When lightning struck Antony church on Whit Sunday 1640, he considered it 'the Voice of the Lord in the Temple: or a most strange and wonderful relation of God's great power, providence and mercy, in sending very strange sounds, fires, and a fiery ball into the church of Antony, to the scorching and astonishing of 14 several persons who were smitten'. Two years later a far greater storm broke – the Civil War – which was to sweep away the next generation of the Carews.

Civil wars divide families as well as nations. Among the more dissolute members of the Cavalier court had been Richard's cousin, the poet Thomas Carew, whose flowery celebration of sex, *A Rapture*, was published in 1640. Although Richard himself was made a baronet by Charles I the following year, his puritan faith inclined him to the Parliamentary cause. Both his sons, Alexander, who succeeded him as 2nd Baronet in 1643, and John, were from the start firm opponents of the Crown. Alexander Carew represented the county in the Long Parliament, and, when his Cornish colleague, the royalist Sir Bevel Grenville, tried to dissuade

Richard Carew; by an unknown English artist, 1586 (Hall)

him from supporting the bill for the Earl of Strafford's execution, he is said to have replied, 'If I were sure to be the next man that should suffer upon the same scaffold with the same axe, I would give my consent to the passing of it'. At the outbreak of war he was chosen to raise the Cornish militia against the King, and given command of the strategic island of St Nicholas guarding the approaches to Plymouth, the parliamentary strong-

Sir Alexander Carew; by an unknown English artist, c.1630 (Library). During the Civil War he supported the Parliamentary side – to the fury of some of his family, who are said to have slashed his portrait from its frame. The picture still bears the scars

hold in the West Country. According to tradition, Sir Alexander's stand so enraged the royalist members of his family that they slashed his portrait from its frame and consigned it to the cellars of Antony.

In the early months things did not go well for the Parliamentary cause in the West Country. As Prince Maurice marched victoriously through Somerset towards Plymouth, Sir Alexander began to wonder whether he was on the right side. The cynical Clarendon wrote that Carew 'understood the law so well (for he had a good education) to know, that the side he had chosen would be no longer the better than it should continue the stronger.' Carew passed a message via his royalist cousin, Colonel Piers Edgcumbe, to the commander of the King's forces before Exeter, offering to surrender Sir Nicholas Island to him. However, he wanted binding assurances of his safety from the King, and while he was waiting for these to arrive he was betrayed by a servant. Taken by sea to London, he was condemned to death and on 23 December 1644 beheaded on Tower Hill. His speech from the scaffold is recorded in a contemporary pamphlet. It makes unhappy reading, for he was clearly a broken man. He embraced death 'with unfeigned desire and hearty affection', but did so without the consolation of a clear conscience. His last thoughts were of his family: he directed the headsman, 'When I say, "Lord, though thou killest me, yet will I put my trust in thee," then thou cut off my head; for it was the last words that ever my mother spoke when she died'. Despite Sir Alexander's doubts, his death took on the character of a martyrdom for his royalist kinsmen, who are said to have rescued his portrait from the cellars and restored it to its frame. It hangs in the Library today, and the crude stitches with which it was sewn in again are still visible.

By contrast, Sir Alexander's younger halfbrother, John, never wavered in his convictions. He was appointed one of the King's judges at his trial and signed the death warrant. However, as a devout Fifth Monarchist, he opposed anything that smacked of temporal monarchy, and so attacked Cromwell when he declared himself Lord Protector. He was imprisoned in St Mawes Castle in 1655, but was released and retired to Antony. At

Charles I at his Trial; by Edward Bower, 1648 (Hall).
Both Sir Alexander and John Carew were also executed for
their part in the Civil War

THE BUILDING OF ANTONY

Antony as we see it today was very largely the creation of one man, Sir William Carew (1689–1744), the 5th Baronet. The youngest of Sir John Carew's seven children, he would not, in the normal way of things, have expected to inherit either the estate or the means to build such a grand new home. However, the lottery of birth and death intervened. Sir John's first two marriages produced only daughters (including the Rachel Carew on whom Daphne du Maurier based, very loosely, *My Cousin Rachel*). By his third wife Sir John finally sired an heir, Richard, who was briefly the 4th Baronet, but died young and unmarried in 1703, leaving his younger brother, William to succeed.

Coming of age in 1710, William Carew looked about him for a wife. He had known Anne Coventry, the granddaughter of one of his Edgcumbe kin, since childhood; in 1712 her prospects

Sir William Carew, 5th Bt, the builder of Antony; by
Michael Dahl (Main Stairs)

the Restoration in 1660 he voluntarily surrendered himself to Parliament, calmly enduring the taunts of the mob, who cried, 'This is the rogue who will have no king but Jesus'. He was convicted at the Old Bailey of regicide, and executed at Charing Cross on 15 October 1660, facing death 'with great composure of mind'. His body was then stripped naked, hacked into quarters and dragged back through the streets to Newgate Gaol. Only then were his remains returned to his family for burial.

The Carew baronetcy was inherited by Sir Alexander's eldest surviving son, John (1635–92), who was too young to take any part in the Civil War. A moderate Presbyterian, he represented Cornwall in the Convention Parliament of 1660, which restored Charles II, and helped to bring tranquillity back to the county after the traumas of the previous 20 years.

suddenly and unexpectedly improved. For she was the only daughter and heir of Gilbert Coventry, who, following the deaths in rapid succession of his elder brother and nephew, found himself, in January 1712 (1711 by the old reckoning), 4th Earl of Coventry and a rich man. The date '1711' is cast in lead over the central doorway on the north front of Antony. It seems not to relate to the building of the new house, which did not begin for another six years and it is possible that it commemorates the moment when the Carew fortunes were transformed. In the autumn of 1712 the 4th Earl visited Antony, and marriage between William and Anne was arranged, with an annual jointure of £500. The following year they wed.

William Carew seems to have turned his attention first to the garden. Already in the late 1700s manure was arriving by the bargeload at Antony quay to sweeten the soil. On 6 July 1713 he signed an agreement with the Lambeth nurseryman Humphry Bowen to build a new garden 575 by 254 feet. In October the same year the Exeter master-builder John Moyle was called in to construct the garden walls, and to fire on site the 400,000 bricks needed. Work appears to have begun the following spring. However, in 1715 Carew suffered two setbacks. Firstly, his father-in-law, ten years a widower, unexpectedly decided to remarry. It was fortunate for the Carews that there were no sons of the marriage to rob them of their inheritance, although Anne's stepmother proved a continual trial. More seriously, Carew was arrested as a suspected Jacobite, imprisoned in the citadel at Plymouth and only released on bail in February 1716, when the threat from the 'Old Pretender' had passed. Despite the fate of his grandparents' generation, the dangers of renewed civil war seem not to have worried Carew, who was a lifelong supporter of the exiled Stuarts. After his release he remained in touch with Jacobite agents in France in the 1720s, and was involved in plans for a French landing to restore the Stuarts in 1744, but did not live to see the 'Young Pretender' make his final bid for the British throne the following year.

The Hanoverian succession deprived Carew of any chance of political preferment, and so, like many other Tory landowners, he devoted his time

Lady Anne Coventry; attributed to Michael Dahl (Hall). She married Sir William Carew in 1713, and her inheritance helped to pay for the building of Antony

to building. In 1718 Moyle contracted to erect the shell of a new house 'according to a draught agreed upon in a good workman like manner, and to the satisfaction of Sir William Carew'. The following year the 4th Earl died, and after a certain amount of legal argument from his widow, the Coventry inheritance came to the Carews. Despite temporary financial problems caused by the bursting of the South Sea Bubble in 1720, Carew proceeded apace with his new house. In 1721 stone from Pentewan quarry at St Austell Bay arrived by sea to clad the brick carcass: the date '1721' carved above the north front door may mark the completion of the shell. In January 1722 the painter Robert Riddle sent in his bill. In March 1724 the Plymouth glazier George Carter enquired when glass for the garret windows would be needed. The staircase was paid for in April 1724, and in the same year the rooms were measured up for wainscoting. The Carews moved in shortly afterwards.

On 19 October 1727 the amateur draftsman of country-house views, Edmund Prideaux, paid a brief visit to Antony, and he has left us three invaluable drawings of William Carew's new home. They show the house standing on an airy site on the Antony peninsula. It looks north over an elaborate formal garden of terraced parterres and tree-lined avenues to the estuary of the River Lynher below. To the north-east of the house is the contemporary circular dovecote, which is still a feature of the garden. The public entrance front faces south, away from the estuary. Curiously, despite its geographical proximity to Devon and the Plymouth dockyards, Antony has always been very much a Cornish house, and the Carews an army, rather than a navy, family. (The real-life Admiral Carew, under whom

Horatio Hornblower served as an anxious midshipman, was not related.)

In choosing the design of his new house, the Jacobite Carew looked back nostalgically to the heyday of the Stuarts and to the influential Clarendon House, built by Charles II's Lord Chancellor in Piccadilly in the 1660s. Antony comes at the very end of that tradition and shows it refined to its absolute essentials. The house is no more than a rectangular box of two principal storeys, nine bays by five. The three-bay pediments on the north and south fronts are without cartouches or other embellishments, the windows entirely without entablatures. The cornice, broad string course and simple rusticated quoins are equally severe. It is entirely in character that the pilasters flanking the central door on the north front should be Tuscan, the plainest of the five orders. The beauty of Antony derives not from ornament, but from its stone, which glows a silvery grey on a bright Cornish day, and from its perfect proportions, which give it a strangely timeless quality.

William Carew's garden in 1727, as sketched by Edmund Prideaux

An early 18th-century panorama of Antony
(family museum)

The plan of Antony also harks back to the 17th century and to 'double-pile' houses like Belton in Lincolnshire: two symmetrical ranges of rooms set back-to-back, around an Entrance Hall and Saloon (originally called the Best Parlour), and divided by a spinal corridor running the entire length of the house. The arrangement is most obvious on the first floor, where the corridor has survived intact. Minor changes have since been made on the ground floor, but this plan has proved itself remarkably adaptable over three centuries.

More modern in style are the two brick pavilions, which flank the south front of the house and are connected to it by arcaded passages to create a forecourt, whose corners are enlivened by strangely pagoda-like cupolas. Prideaux's 1727 drawing of this front shows the pavilions and arcades, but not the wall and gates which still form the south side of the forecourt. These must have been added shortly afterwards, for they appear in an anonymous, undated, but early 18th-century view, which also records a figure sculpture standing on a substantial plinth in the centre of the forecourt. (The sculpture had gone by 1758, when William Borlase engraved his view.)

Who designed this remarkable ensemble? Moyle, the builder, worked at Boconnoc House for Thomas Pitt, and at Powderham Castle in Devon for Sir William Courtenay, and was probably capable of producing his own designs. Unfortunately, there is no evidence that he ever did, and the implication of the 1718 contract seems to be that he was working to another's plan. There is a tradition dating back at least to the Lysons' *Magna Britannia* of 1814 that the architect was James Gibbs. Moreover, plate 57 of Gibbs's *Book of Architecture* illustrates the plan and elevation of 'a house designed for a gentleman in the country', which is strikingly similar to Antony. Gibbs's house has three principal storeys to Antony's two, and the central bays are heavily rusticated, but in other respects they match, and the treatment and dimensions of the colonnaded forecourt and pavilions are almost identical. Gibbs's book was intended to be 'of use to such gentlemen as might be concerned in building, especially in the remote parts of the country, where little or no assistance for designs can be procured'. Carew certainly fell into that category of gentlemen, and in several other respects he was eminently qualified to be patron of Gibbs. He was a Tory, and Tory landowners favoured Gibbs. He subscribed to the *Book of Architecture,* and had his portrait painted by Dahl, a member of the Gibbs circle. Another Gibbs intimate, the horse painter John Wootton, was patronised by Carew's father-in-law, who was something of a connoisseur. However, Gibbs's book did not appear until 1728, and so, in its published form at least, can hardly have provided the pattern for Antony. Besides, Gibbs is not known to have worked so far west, his name is nowhere recorded in the considerable Antony muniments, and the plain, panelled interiors of the house are, apart from the marble chimney-piece in the Tapestry Room, very unGibbsian in style.

The current consensus is this. The main block was put up first, to the design of a still unidentified architect perhaps with some knowledge of contemporary government buildings in the Plymouth dockyards. Subsequently, Gibbs proposed enlivening the severity of the original design by rusticating the central three bays, raising another storey and

Sir Coventry Carew, 6th Bt; attributed to John Wootton (Main Stairs)

adding the flanking pavilions and arcaded forecourt. For lack of money or some other reason, Carew did nothing to the house, contenting himself with building the pavilions and forecourt in cheaper brick. Whatever the exact sequence of events, the result was the finest house of its period in Cornwall.

On Sir William's death in 1744, his only son, Coventry (1716?–48) became the 6th Baronet. Sir Coventry died only four years later without a son, at which point the Carew baronetcy went to cousins. After the death of Sir Coventry's widow, Mary, before 1763, the estate devolved on the Crowcombe branch of the Carew family, going first to Thomas and then John Carew (1734–71). This is a hazy period in the history of Antony, but an agreement dated 1768 between John Carew and the gardener, Philip Langdon, captures something of the flavour of life at Antony in the 1760s. In Carew's absence Langdon was 'to provide the servants with all manner of kitchen and garden stuff (the wall fruit and table fruit saved for Mr Carew with all things from the garden when the family was in residence). He was to have use of garden produce for himself, to leave all in good order, not to diminish any of the trees, etc., and to have meat and drink in the house.'

LATER HISTORY

In accordance with Sir Coventry Carew's Will, in 1772 the estate passed to Reginald Pole (1753–1835). The great-great-grandson through the female line of the 3rd Baronet, Sir John Carew. (The descent is traced on the family tree on the inside back cover.) Pole had been brought up at Stoke Damerel just across the Tamar from Antony, so must already have known the house well. He adopted the surname Pole-Carew on inheriting Antony, and set off on the Grand Tour. In 1773 he was in Besançon where his profile was painted by Wyrsch; he seems not to have returned to Cornwall until 1781. The powerful support of Pole-Carew's neighbour, Lord Mount Edgcumbe, and the Hardwicke connections of his first wife Jemima Yorke, ensured him a seat in Parliament. He was

MP for Fowey for many years, but appears to have lacked self-confidence and found the politician's life irksome. As he wrote to his brother in 1799, 'The early dinners, the late dinners, the no dinners, and the great dinners of the House of Commons I have always found as adverse to health as inconsistent with all domestic comfort.'

Pole-Carew preferred to devote himself to improving his substantial inheritance. He was much involved in developing the new town of Torpoint, inaugurating the Torpoint Ferry in 1790 with the 1st Earl of Mount Edgcumbe. On the Antony estate he built the Bath House beside the River Lynher in 1788–90, to a design by Thomas Parlby. In the late 1780s he began ordering forest, fruit and ornamental trees in prodigious quantities, together with shrubs, and flower and vegetable seeds. Growing increasingly ambitious, in 1792 Pole-Carew sought the advice of Humphry Repton, who was then just starting out on a prolific career that was to transform the landscape gardens of Britain. At a cost of 30 guineas Repton produced one of his famous

Reginald Pole-Carew; by Wyrsch, 1773 (West Stairs)

Red Books. Pole-Carew was entranced, writing on 20 December 1792, 'I was up to twelve at night, and could not go to sleep until I thoroughly examined the treasure you put in my hands.'

Repton's proposals were typically radical. The approach from the south was unsatisfactory. A lodge should mark the point where the visitor entered the grounds from the local turnpike. The drive should not be unduly drawn out, but be planted so as to conceal the south front of the house until it could tell to best advantage. The wall enclosing the south forecourt should be demolished to increase this initial impact; the pavilions be raised an extra storey to match the central block, and be rendered the same colour. The garden north and east of the house was too encumbered with gloomy walls; the formal parterres and kitchen garden must go in order to create smooth, grassy vistas down to the river. A new kitchen garden should be built to the west of the house.

Pole-Carew remained on amicable terms with Repton for almost 20 years, but his initial enthusiasm seems to have given way to caution. New lodges were built, probably by Repton's son, John Adey Repton, and the old parterres and kitchen garden removed. The new walled kitchen garden was built on Higher West Down by the Milanese architect Placido Columbani, who also designed a new London house for him in 1801, at 7 New Cavendish Street on the Portland estate. (His London residence for the previous 16 years had been in Charles Street, Berkeley Square.) However, neither the approach nor the south forecourt were altered, and Pole-Carew largely pleased himself in laying out his woodlands, although he accepted the importance of creating vistas from the house. Pole-Carew's eldest son by his first marriage, Joseph (1787–1852), inherited in 1835 and died 17 years later, having produced no male heirs and having left little mark on Antony. The estate passed to his half-brother, William Henry (1811–88). Antony House was by then over 100 years old and did not meet mid-Victorian standards of comfort and convenience. To make the Hall less draughty and keep the rain off arriving visitors, William Henry added a glazed outer hall and pedimented *porte-cochère* to the south front. Alas, this unwieldy

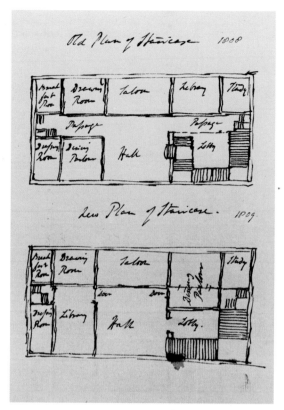

Reginald Pole-Carew's sketches for remodelling the ground floor in 1808–9. The old 'dining parlour' was extended to become the present Library. The bottom flight of the Main Stairs was removed and the present Dining Room enlarged to take in part of the Inner Hall. (The south wall of the Dining Room was later returned to its original position)

protuberance robs the Hall of light and spoils the delicate proportions of the entrance front. (If William Henry had consulted his ancestor's copy of Gibbs's *Book of Architecture*, he would have found in plate 58 a more elegant solution to the problem: an open loggia with a recessed doorway screen behind.) It was probably about this time that a modest two-storey wing was also added to the east of the house to provide more accommodation for the growing number of guests and servants. Old photographs show it to have been a simple Italianate style popular in the mid-19th century.

William Henry lived long enough to see the plantations laid out by his father reach maturity. He also added new copses here and there, and seems to have been responsible for planting the yew hedges which still line the terrace to the west of the house. He also brought Repton's kitchen garden nearer the house by extending it to the east. Like every conscientious Victorian landowner, he was concerned for the spiritual and educational needs of his tenants. He built the School House at Maryfield in 1847 and the nearby church of SS Philip and James in 1866 as a thanksgiving for the birth of his children.

William Henry was MP for East Cornwall from 1845 to 1852 and active in county affairs. His son, Reginald Pole-Carew (1849-1924), had a brilliant military career on an altogether wider stage. He joined the Coldstream Guards as a young ensign in 1869 and by the time he retired in 1906 was a major-general. During the Second Afghan War (1878–80) he served as ADC to the greatest of all

A bust of William Henry Pole-Carew stands in the Entrance Porch

37

The south front, with the porte-cochère added in the mid-19th century by William Henry Pole-Carew

the Victorian generals, Frederick Roberts, who considered 'Polly Carew', as he affectionately called him, 'a nice well plucked fellow'. Pole-Carew had to show all his pluck during the epic march from Kabul to Kandahar in 1880. In 24 days 10,000 men marched 320 miles across the mountainous and hostile territory of the North-West Frontier to save the beleaguered British garrison. Pole-Carew completed the journey despite being seriously ill. Subsequently, he fought in Egypt and the Second Burmese War, and again under Roberts throughout the Boer War. Having commanded the Guards Brigade with distinction at the Battle of Modder River in November 1899, he was given his own Division (the 11th), which he led through the rest of the South African campaign. He was twice mentioned in despatches and knighted on his return. Although 70 when the First World War broke out in 1914, he offered his services to Lord Kitchener, who appointed him Inspector-General of the Territorial Forces. However, a serious riding accident the following year finally brought his military career to an end.

Despite long periods abroad, Sir Reginald still found time to consider improvements to Antony. Sir William Carew's house lacked large public rooms for entertaining the county and that essential requirement of the late Victorian gentleman – a billiard room. To provide these, it must have seemed an attractive idea to remodel the unassuming east wing in the style of Trerice, the family home of his distant ancestor, Juliana Arundell. Unfortunately, the result – in red brick with fussy gables – looked more like a Pont Street Dutch mansion block than an ancient Cornish manor house. It also clashed horribly with the grey stone of the main building and destroyed its simple symmetry. The work was completed in 1905 while Sir Reginald was away serving in Ireland. He is said to have been appalled when he returned to discover what had been done, remarking that his son would no doubt pull it down.

Sir Reginald had more success in the garden. To the north of the house he restored the early 18th-century parterres and topped the enclosing walls with handsome urns. He also framed the view of the river with a wrought-iron screen and ornamental gates based on a Jacobean set at Beddington in Surrey, the former home of Nicholas Carew, Master of the Horse to Henry VIII. This was Victorian gardening at its most lavish: 27 separate

The north front, showing the wing (on the left) and walled garden added by Sir Reginald Pole-Carew. Both have now gone

One of the Gandharan sculptures brought back by Sir Reginald Pole-Carew from the North-West Frontier

gardens, 400 yards of flower-beds and herbaceous borders, looked after by his wife, Lady Beatrice, and an army of gardeners. Sir Reginald also extended the Yew Walk and closed the vista with a vast bell, a trophy brought back from the Burma Wars. His Gandharan sculptures from the North-West Frontier provided equally eye-catching features in the garden, but recently they have had to be moved indoors to protect them from the frost. He renewed the now-ageing original planting, and around 1913 planned, but never completed, an imposing new approach to the house down an avenue of chestnuts.

Sir Reginald died in 1924; two years later, his son, John (1902–93), took the name Carew Pole on inheriting the ancient baronetcy of Pole of Shute. With the title came the Shute estate near Axminster in Devon, the famous library of manuscripts and books founded by the 17th-century historian Sir William Pole, and many fine family portraits, including the delightful Hudson of the 5th Baronet, Sir John Pole, and his wife, Elizabeth, which now hangs on the stairs at Antony. In 1959 Sir John gave Shute Barton to the National Trust, which leases the detached Elizabethan gatehouse to the Landmark Trust as a holiday cottage.

Antony was further enriched in 1928, when Sir John married Cynthia Burns. For she was a great-niece of the American financier J. P. Morgan, and inherited 18th-century china and furniture from his legendary collection, together with pictures from her aunt, Mrs Arthur James.

Lady Carew Pole had been brought up at North Mymms Park in Hertfordshire, which was famous for its rose garden, and she shared her mother-in-law, Lady Beatrice's love of flowers. Together, the Carew Poles set about improving the garden at Antony. In the early 1930s they were invited to Lionel de Rothschild's pioneering garden of hybrid rhododendrons at Exbury in Hampshire, and were fascinated by what they saw. Following their visit, the stationmaster at North Road, Plymouth, rang to say that two coal-trucks full of plants had arrived from Exbury for them.

For Sir John life at Antony was combined with a military career. He served throughout the inter-war years in the Coldstream Guards, retiring in 1939 to return to Cornwall. Sir John then joined the Territorial Army and was appointed CO of the 5th Battalion of his local regiment, the Duke of Cornwall's Light Infantry. For the next four years he prepared his battalion for combat with a judicious mixture of Brigade of Guards discipline and local understanding.

Before the DCLI could see action, Sir John was posted, in July 1944, to command the 2nd Battalion of the Devonshire Regiment, which was then in the thick of the Normandy campaign. He led the battalion from the woody *bocage* country of Normandy on the rapid advance through Belgium to the liberation of Brussels, and then in the increasingly desperate attempts to reach the British 1st Airborne Division, cut off at Arnhem. Awarded the DSO in November 1944, he served for the rest of the war with the 2nd Army.

In austere post-war Britain Sir Reginald Pole-Carew's east wing was even more out of place than when first built. Sir John commissioned Philip Tilden to remove it and make Antony a more practical house to live in. As Tilden recalled:

Sir John Carew Pole in his army uniform; painted by Oswald Birley in 1944 (First-Floor Corridor)

It was a pleasure to organise the amputation of this disfigurement and restore the house to its former symmetry. The red bricks from the demolition I had buried in a quarry lest anyone should be tempted to re-use them in this district of grey stone and granite. I also replanned the kitchens and simplified the gardens so that both could be run with less labour, and converted the service wings into self-contained flats for employees and relatives.

In 1961 Sir John gave Antony, with 29 acres and an endowment, to the National Trust to ensure its permanent preservation. In 1983 he moved into a smaller house on the estate so that his son, Richard, could live at Antony with his family. Sir Richard Carew Pole is the third generation to have served in the Coldstream Guards and is active in a wide range of county affairs. He recently completed five years as President of the Royal Horticultural Society, and his wife, Mary, is a lady-in-waiting to the Princess Royal. He takes a close interest in everything that happens at Antony, and has restored the 'fishful pond' of his famous Elizabethan ancestor and namesake.